GREAT BUSINESSES YOU CAN START ON A SHOESTRING

DEDICATION

To all those who have made up their minds that
they will never again be dependent on someone
else to provide them with a paycheck.

PROGRESSIVE PUBLICATIONS
P.O. Box 4016
Homosassa Springs, FL 32647
(904) 382-1452   FAX (904) 382-4614

FORWARD

Just about all of us dream of being in our own business. Not having to answer to the whims of those who chart our activities each day sure sounds great. And it definitely can be. However, being self employed can also put you in the position of having the worst boss you have ever had.

Being a successful entrepreneur requires self discipline and just plain hard work. Those who believe they are going to obtain big money while working as few hours as possible will inevitably end up being one of the 70% of all new businesses that fail.

Attitude is the key!

Saying, "Sure, that's OK for people with money, but I don't have the funds to start my own business!" is just not a valid excuse.

The opportunities in this book can all be started with a very modest investment, some without any investment at all.

Make up your mind to do it and do it! There is no reason for anyone to be out of work and helpless.

Can't sell? Don't ever think this again. If you can communicate in any way, you can sell. You may not realize it but all of us sell every day. Selling is simply taking a product we believe in and asking people to buy it.

Regardless of the business we start, we must sell.

Now read this book thoroughly and start calling and writing everyone who can lend you a hand.

You are a success the day you start developing your business plan and say to yourself: "I'm going for it and nobody is going to stop me!"

TABLE OF CONTENTS

CHAPTER 1

SELF EXAMINATION
FOR THOSE CONSIDERING
SELF-EMPLOYMENT

SELF EXAMINATION FOR THOSE CONSIDERING SELF EMPLOYMENT

Although it is the dream of most of us to be in business for ourselves, everyone isn't suited for it.

Just as we are all different in appearance, we are likewise different in our physical chemistry and, as such, our intelligence and personality characteristics are unique.

Despite the fact that all the entrepreneurial opportunities described in this book can be started with very few dollars, that is no reason to believe that the risk is minimal. If your business fails, you lose time, you lose your investment, and you lose your self esteem.

If you carefully assess your possibilities and prepare thoroughly by detailing an exact plan, your chances of success are far more realistic than those who impetuously jump on an idea and work by trial and error.

It is a fact that more than 50% of all new businesses fail within the first year. An additional 20% close within five years.

BE HONEST WITH YOURSELF WHEN ANSWERING THE QUESTIONS BELOW!

1. Are you self confident? Do you feel you can handle any problem which may arise? No business has ever been started where the owners didn't experience problems which never could have been foreseen. Are you mentally tough enough to say to yourself, "No problem, I can handle it!"?

2. Are you an optimist? If you generally are the type of person who wallows in self pity and constantly thinks negatively, then think twice about going into business. This outlook on life is usually the result of programming. However, you can change. Start with a copy of *The Power of Positive Thinking* by Norman Vincent Peale.

3. Are you assertive? Although you can succeed very well without being assertive, it certainly helps to have this characteristic as fewer people will shove you around. Unfortunately, you either are assertive or you are not. You can take assertiveness classes so that you can appear to be assertive, but in reality you don't have a choice.

4. Can you persist towards a goal once you start? Perhaps the greatest attribute you can possess is having the determination to keep on keeping on. If your goal is realistic and you keep working, someday you are going to get there.

If you examine the lives of all great men and women in business, you'll realize that the only reason you know of them is because they never gave up.

Colonel Saunders approached over 1000 restaurants before he got an owner to agree to his recipe for fried chicken.

Tom Monahan failed numerous times before his chain of Domino's Pizza Shops started to gain stability. This year he'll gross over 3 billion dollars.

If you are the type of individual who gives up easily, don't consider starting your own business.

5. Are you generally efficient? Do you have the ability to plan thoroughly? When you tackle a job, do you do things so they are "good enough" or do you insist on pleasing yourself by being more exact, performing to the best of your abilities?

6. Can you listen to others? Communicate with others? If you want to be in your own business because you won't have to listen to anyone, and you can do what you want when you want, you will definitely have a fool for a boss. To succeed, find those who have been successful in businesses similar to the one you want to start. Then ask, ask, ask, and listen, listen, listen.

Most people who fail have not done their homework. It makes no sense whatsoever to make the same mistakes as those who have gone before you. To stubbornly say, "I'll do it my way" is first class stupidity when experience is there for anyone who asks.

If you are not confident about your ability to communicate with others, pick up a copy of *How To Win Friends and Influence People* by Dale Carnegie. This book has sold many millions of copies and for good reason. It's invaluable!

7. Can you organize your time? Once you set a goal and are excited about reaching it, it is important to remain focused on your objective. This can best be accomplished by making a "Things I Must Do Today" list every morning. Include something on that list every day which brings you closer to your major objective.

Once you get in the habit of making this daily list, you will find that you will accomplish more each day than you ever did before.

8. Can you remain honest and dedicated to high standards? To base your future on a foundation of deceit and the old adage, "There's a fool born every minute" is a short cut to bankruptcy court. Today's consumer is well informed and well protected by law.

Gaining a reputation as one who has integrity is money in the bank. Customers who feel they can trust you will always keep your phone number where they can't lose it.

9. Can you make a decision? A good business person is decisive and quick to act. This attribute is essential to being a problem solver. As a matter of fact, the greatest problem solving technique known to man is: "MAKE A DECISION".

Sure, your decision may often be the same as exchanging one problem for another, but consider this: the new problem may be far easier for you to solve than the former.

If you are the type who simply "can't make a decision", then perhaps you are better off working for someone who can.

10. Can you work 80 to 90 hours a week? This, of course, requires having the right attitude. If you don't have it, if you aren't excited about your new business so you don't care how many hours a week you have to work, then don't go any further. You will be much better off working for someone else.

11. Do the others who make up your immediate environment share your dreams? You can't do your best at any endeavor unless you are happy. And you sure can't be happy if you have a spouse who is constantly complaining about what you are doing or the hours you are putting in. Your friends and associates should also share your enthusiasm and be supportive rather than negative.

The choice you have is to proceed only with the blessings of those in your immediate environment, or change your environment completely so that you surround yourself with positive support.

12. Is your business objective well conceived and realistically believable? Wishing won't make it so. Even though you are sold on the "can't miss" concept offered in the formula for success, all aspects of a plan must be realistic.

A well conceived business that may work great in Portland may be a disaster in Poughkeepsie. Do your research well. Ask yourself if you will have sufficient funds to get over the hill. Ask yourself if you have left anything out of your plan on paper. And by all means go out and ask the opinions of those who will make up your list of customers.

Only if you believe you will succeed, will you succeed. If you have doubts, do not proceed.

> **"A man to carry on a successful business must have imagination. He must see things as in a vision, a dream of the whole thing."**
>
> **Charles M. Schwab**

CHAPTER 2

A FEW MORE THINGS
YOU SHOULD KNOW

A FEW MORE THINGS YOU SHOULD KNOW

Only 30% of all new businesses will still be around five years after they are started. Poor planning is almost always the culprit. Your plan must be thorough. Here are a few good points we want you to understand and consider carefully!

1. IF YOU CANNOT READ AND WRITE AS WELL AS YOU SHOULD, LEARN HOW BEFORE YOU DO ANYTHING ELSE.

Check your local community for courses.

For home-study classes in English, contact one of the following schools:

American School
850 East 58th Street
Chicago, IL 60637

Citizen's High School
5115 New Peachtree Road, Suite 300
Atlanta, GA 30341

English Language Institute of America
332 South Michigan Avenue, Suite 1058
Chicago, IL 60604

Home Study International
P.O. Box 4437
Silver Spring, MD 20914-4437

ICS-Newport/Pacific High School
Scranton, PA 18515

For English courses for Spanish speaking people, write:

Hemphill Schools
510 S. Alvarado Street
Los Angeles, CA 90057-2998

2. KNOW BASIC MATH. EVERY BUSINESS REQUIRES IT. EVERY ONE!

Check your local community for courses.

For home-study courses in Mathematics, contact one of the following schools:

American School
850 East 58th Street
Chicago, IL 60637

Citizen's High School
5115 New Peachtree Road, Suite 300
Atlanta, GA 30341

Home Study International
P.O. Box 4437
Silver Spring, MD 20914-4437

International Correspondence Schools
Scranton, PA 18515

3. FIND A GOOD ACCOUNTANT AND A GOOD ATTORNEY WHO SPECIALIZE IN SMALL BUSINESS.

If you can't afford to spend money for their advice before you start your business, consider offering them stock in your corporation. Then have the attorney set up the corporation after your accountant advises you which type of corporation is best for you. (Covered in Chapter 5.)

Don't just pick names out of the yellow pages. Keep asking other businessmen if they could recommend their attorneys and accountants.

What you want to find are professionals who can assist you with the future, not just those who can accurately report on the past or tell you what you should not have done.

4. PERFORM MARKET ANALYSIS BEFORE YOU SPEND A DIME TO START YOUR NEW BUSINESS.

You can't just assume you will have buyers for your products or services. Find out. Get out of your house and start talking to those who you believe to be your future clients. Ask them: "Would you buy my products and/or services?" If not, ask: "Why not?", then: "Under what circumstances or conditions would you buy my products and/or services?"

Write down every response as you hear it. Keep asking and writing until what you must do becomes clear in your mind.

5. LEARN FROM THE EXPERIENCE OF OTHERS.

If you already have a burning desire to open a specific type of business, great! But don't make the mistake so many hardheads make by stubbornly insisting, "I'll do it my way. I don't need advice." Take the time to go talk to those who have succeeded in a similar business, regardless if it means driving 3,000 miles to get there. Ask for their opinions, suggestions and thoughts. If you aren't a competitive threat, chances are they will be glad to assist you. Stay there and listen as long as you can. Write everything down.

If you don't know what business to go into (only that you are destined to be your own boss), we suggest you become an ardent listener. Wherever you go, make a practice of writing down every complaint you hear. The more complaints you record about a single subject, the greater the market will be for those seeking a solution.

When you have settled on an idea that keeps you lying awake at night and fully excited every hour of the day, perhaps it is time to proceed. But again, go talk to those who have already met success with an idea similar to yours. Whether your idea is in service, manufacturing, retailing or otherwise, someone somewhere has unique experiences you can benefit from. Find these people and ask for their help.

6. IF YOU ARE STARTING A BUSINESS SIMILAR TO OTHERS, MAKE YOURS UNIQUELY BETTER!

Thousands of companies have produced beautiful dolls, yet the homely Cabbage Patch Kids will go down in history with sales over two billion. They were the product of a junior college dropout by the name of Xavier Roberts. He figured out a way, with the use of a computer, to make each one different. He then devised the marketing gimmick that produced the phenomenon: giving each a name and a birth certificate.

How many pizza shops do you suppose there are in this country that deliver a pretty good product? Thousands? At least, and yet Tom Monaghan took Domino's Pizza to national prominence with one significant idea that others didn't use. Delivery within thirty minutes . . . guaranteed! This year Domino's sales will exceed three billion.

If you intend to succeed as few others, then you must think as few others. Answer the question, "What will I do that the others won't do, or can't do?" Be one of a kind!

7. LEARN HOW TO HIRE, TRAIN, AND MOTIVATE BEFORE YOU EVER BECOME AN EMPLOYER.

If you expect to expand your business beyond what you are able to do yourself, you must begin to hire people to work for you. Knowing who, how, and when to hire can make you or break you.

I have personally made hiring mistakes on different occasions that almost bankrupt three different corporations. I thought I certainly knew how to choose a winner; nobody was going to fool me. Boy, was I wrong. This naive attitude cost me in excess of $70,000.00 plus the price of aspirin, tranquilizers and Pepto-Bismol.

Before you say yes to anyone you intend to hire, check them out! Don't be hasty because you need someone right away. Be thorough! Check every reference and, if possible, go to their home and see how they live.

You are taking a risk every time you add someone to your payroll, as they become part of the image of your company.

To receive a complete catalog of personnel products and publications, contact:

Borgman Associates
321 Lennon Lane
Walnut Creek, CA 94598-2435
Phone 1-800-942-4494

8. STUDY ADVERTISING AND MARKETING

Regardless of the business you intend to enter, you must be a sales person. You can't sell, you say! Nonsense.

Having "a gift of gab" is by no means necessary. If we were to profile the attributes of this country's greatest salespeople, the most common characteristics would be:

a) They all sell a product or service they believe in and enjoy offering.

b) They all possess the self-discipline to work a regimented number of hours every week.

c) They all ask people to buy and persist in follow-up if any chance for a sale is deemed possible.

d) They all understand that all good selling is serving, and that people buy benefits.

Selling in advertising is much the same as what a sales person might say in person, but don't assume you know how to write a good ad or commercial. Go to the library and take out books to school yourself in this subject.

9. EXPECT PROBLEMS, . . . EXPECT TO HANDLE THEM

With thorough planning, daily as well as long-range, you will avoid numerous problems that could otherwise disable you. No amount of forethought however, will eliminate all adversity. Things will go wrong. And while you can't plan so that you will have no difficulties, you can plan to be tough and unbending when the black clouds hover overhead.

Right here and now, I am going to give you the "Greatest Problem Solving Technique" known to man. It is just this: "MAKE A DECISION."

You see, most problems remain emotionally painful because the problem bearers continue to allow them to exist unchanged. Now, I am not suggesting here that you will always make the right decision which will allow you to live happily ever after, but as soon as you make any decision, the original problem no longer exists.

Can you go from the frying pan into the fire? Of course! But forethought can usually prevent creating a worse problem than you had to begin with. The key here is to think and act. Don't procrastinate.

Before you start into business, say to yourself, "I don't care what adversity comes my way, I am going to handle it." Having this attitude provides the strength that allows you to be a winner.

Years ago I knew a very successful real estate broker by the name of Jim Hulett. I'll never forget him, for he was the first person I ever knew who claimed, "I love problems." At hearing this I felt sure he was putting me on, but he wasn't. He was serious. His explanation made sense, so much so, that I am repeating it here.

"Winners do things that others don't do. When I solve a problem that others won't tackle, I'm a winner. Winners live exciting lives. When I don't have a problem to solve, I don't have the opportunity to be a winner. A racetrack sure isn't exciting when no races are run. I sure like problems."

10. YOU CANNOT FAIL IF YOU ADHERE TO THE "FORMULA FOR SUCCESS"

Throughout the entire history of mankind, it has become apparent that those extraordinary men and women who are renowned for their accomplishments, all had something in common: a plan that included five major points. We pass them on to you here. Use them with all your might and you cannot fail. Only one prerequisite is necessary: your goal must be realistically believable.

"Anything the Mind Can Conceive, and Believe, Can be Achieved!"

If you intend to succeed at anything in your lifetime, you must plan.

IF YOU INTEND TO, HERE ARE THE FIVE POINTS OF THE SUCCESS FORMULA

1. ESTABLISH A BELIEVABLE GOAL. WRITE IT DOWN.

Be specific about the details of your plan and record the date when you intend to accomplish your goal. It is necessary to provide a "DEADLINE" for yourself.

2. VISUALIZE YOURSELF ALREADY HAVING ACCOMPLISHED YOUR GOAL.

We become what we think about. Throughout each day, you must continually take the time to dream. The more you concentrate on what it will be like when your goal is realized, the more the details of your plan will fall into place. To keep this idea alive, we suggest you make a "THINGS I MUST DO TODAY" list every day from now on. Do this either at night before retiring or the first thing in the morning. After you get in the habit of doing this, you will find that you will accomplish twice as much in the course of your working day.

3. MAINTAIN A POSITIVE ATTITUDE.

We suggest three methods:

a) Associate only with those who also are optimists. Rid your environment of those pessimists who constantly say "I CAN'T", or who tell you "YOU'LL NEVER DO IT." Share your dreams with your positive thinking friends.

b) Use a concept which many have titled "AUTOSUGGESTION." It is simply the procedure of repeating a positive statement over and over again. The mind is capable of amazing feats. Somehow it allows us to be what we think about if we continually make a statement. Muhammed Ali transformed himself into the Heavyweight Champion of the World by repeating "I AM THE GREATEST." Tom Monaghan brought his struggling Domino's Pizza Company to world prominence by saying "I AM GOING TO BE THE BEST PIZZA MAKER IN THE WORLD." Try it. It works.

c) Take 15 minutes a day to read some self-improvement books. There are many of them on the market, but to get started try *The Power Of Positive Thinking* by Norman Vincent Peale, or *Think and Grow Rich* by Napoleon Hill. They are two of the best and you shouldn't have any difficulty finding them at any library or bookstore.

4. PERSEVERE. DON'T ALLOW YOURSELF TO GIVE UP.

Sure, you will encounter problems, but refuse to let them get you down. Have the courage to pick yourself up after every set-back, readjust your plan, and start again. Remember that failure is a great teacher, and that *"In every adversity, there is the equivalent of an equal or greater benefit."* If you maintain this attitude you ultimately will succeed. Almost all failures that occur are the result of somebody's giving up or not being adequately prepared for the battle. Persevere.

WORK-WORK-WORK-WORK-WORK

You can't very well dream up clever ways to make a million and then work a six hour day implementing your ideas. Nothing is that simple. If you want to succeed, forget about working average hours. There is a price to pay and it is an unrelenting, uncompromising, uncommon effort.

CHAPTER 3
CHOOSING A BUSINESS THAT "TURNS YOU ON"

CHOOSING A BUSINESS THAT "TURNS YOU ON"

On the following pages you will find descriptions of numerous opportunities for those of you who honesty believe you are well suited for the life of an entrepreneur.

What is unique about these businesses is that they all can be started for a very small dollar investment.

What is also significant is that all these businesses can be operated out of your own home. No rental of buildings is necessary.

We suggest that you read all the ideas presented here and while doing so write down your thoughts. Make notes on those businesses which hold your interest.

After reading this entire book, start following up every source if further information on that one opportunity which most "turns you on".

Most of all, we suggest that you dream, dream, dream. As noted in the "Formula For Success" you have just read in Chapter 2, you should be able to visualize yourself performing every aspect of your new business.

If you find yourself constantly thinking about one single business and admit that you can't get it out of your mind, you are well on your way to a successful future.

Only if you are truly excited about an idea for being self-employed, and are confident, should you proceed. Just because you can see how a business can bring in great money is not a good enough reason to begin. It is an absolute must that you enjoy your occupation.

Your objective now is to find that opportunity which will bring you happiness. A million dollars means nothing if your life is miserable. And of course it is a fact that you can only excel at an endeavor if you like what you are doing.

> **"Destiny is no matter of chance. It is a matter of choice: It is not a thing to be waited for, it is a thing to be achieved."**
>
> **William Jennings Bryan**

AEROSAL TEAR GAS SALES

We think this is a great product for you to start with as we believe the manufacturer is sound, the product has been tested and found reliable, and the market has barely been touched.

You can, in effect, be a manufacturer's rep for an initial investment of just $75.00, plus the minimum cost of one dozen Pocket-Purse units at about $50.00.

A unit that costs you about $4.00 is sold for about $12.00. Being a master distributor also allows you the freedom to set your own wholesale prices so you can sell to others who will in turn sell them at retail prices.

Two sizes are offered. The larger unit will shoot a stream of alpha-chloroacetophenone 15 to 25 feet. It can be used for 60 one-second bursts and has a storage life of two years.

The smaller (pocket-purse) unit shoots a stream 10 to 15 feet and holds approximately 25 one-second bursts.

The gas emitted will immobilize anyone for approximately 15 minutes, during which time the individual affected will be temporarily blinded and have a strong temptation to cover his face with both hands.

This product is used by many police departments throughout the United States.

For complete details call or write:

Hankins Marketing Corporation
128 North Merritt Avenue
Salisbury, NC 28144
Phone (704) 637-3589.

ALARM SYSTEMS

Few opportunities which you can get into for a small investment have such enormous potential.

Factually, this is perhaps the only legitimate way you will ever have of proving that crime does pay.

According to the National Burglar & Fire Alarm Association, fewer than 25% of businesses and 10% of all homes have any type of fire or burglar alarm. This leaves you with more prospects than you can ever handle as there isn't anyone these days who wouldn't appreciate having more protection.

Another reason this business is a timely one is cost. Just a few years ago, the only people who could afford a security system were the rich. Today, this is simply not so. Technology and the variety of devices on the market has brought prices to within almost everyone's reach.

In addition to fire and burglar alarms for homes and businesses, we now have personal security devices, elaborate autmobile security systems, medical alert devices, parking lot security sytems, children alert systems, etc.

If you have a good understanding of electronics, and like it, then go the the library and ask where you can find the Thomas Register. This is a multiple volume set of books which contain the names, addresses and phone numbers of just about every manufacturer and supplier in the United States.

Look up Alarm Systems. It will be in Volume 1. In the 1990 set, you will find 19 pages of listings from page 431 to 450. Record all companies which produce products you believe you would like to sell. Then write or call for more information.

Once you have acquired the products you intend to market, have materials professionally printed so they are an indication to others that your company is one of quality and integrity.

At that point you then have to interest clients in your products. Say yes to the Yellow Pages, and occasionally run some newspaper ads, but for the most part we suggest you contact Fraternal Organizations, Church Groups, Anti-Crime Organizations, PTA Organizations, etc., and volunteer to provide an interesting demonstration on "Protection Devices Available Today."

Chances are you will have plenty of business without spending much more than the cost of a few gallons of gas.

Now if you know nothing about electronics but would like to learn, write or call for a catalog:

National Association of Trade & Technical Schools
2251 Wisconsin Avenue, N.W.
Washington, D.C. 20007
Phone (202) 333-1021

It is likely that there will be an accredited Electronics School which is not far from you.

A PUBLICATION WORTH THE COST OF A SUBSCRIPTION:

Security Distributing & Marketing Magazine
1350 E. Touhy Avenue
Des Plains, IL 60018
Phone (312) 635-8800

CONTACT THESE ORGANIZATIONS REGARDING MEMBERSHIP AND BENEFITS:

National Alarm Association Of America (Security)
14 South Cass Avenue
Westmont, IL 60559-1864
Phone (708) 810-1474

National Burglar & Fire Alarm Association
7101 Wisconsin Avenue, No. 1390
Bethesda, MD 20814
Phone (301) 907-3202

Publish a monthly "News & Views" magazine.

"No person who is enthusiastic about his work has anything to fear from life."

Samuel Goldwyn

ALCOHOL BREATH ANALYZER MACHINE SALES

Almost every state is now cracking down on drunk drivers as never before. In addition, those bar owners who allow people to drink excessively and then drive are being held accountable. For these reasons, machines which test blood alcohol levels are being accepted, coast to coast.

If you feel you can talk to bar and restaurant owners and tell them how a machine of this type can make them additional money, you can start your own business for less than $2000.00

For more information, call or write all of the following companies. Then you can make a decision based on comparisons.

American Alcohol Chek
8900 Shoal Creek Boulevard, Suite 129
Austin, Texas 78758
(512) 459-3151.

Patriot Alcohol Testers
130 Rockland Street
Hanover, MA 02339
(617) 826-5969.

Communidyne, Inc.
636 Anthony Trail
Northbrook, IL 60062
1-800-637-8363 or (708) 498-2444.

AUCTION BUSINESS

If you like variety, excitement, and don't mind working long hours, this business can be both fun and very profitable.

First of all, you should know how to run an auction, and if you don't have a good friend in this business, then we suggest you go to school. You'll have your choice of two fine schools:

The Missouri Auction School
1600 Genesee
Kansas City, MO 64102
Phone (816) 421-7117

World Wide College Of Auctioneering
P.O. Box 949
15564 300th Street
Mason City, IA 50401
Phone (515) 423-5242.

They will be pleased to send you information on their courses, the tuition, and the available housing. Both of these schools offer short programs which are comprehensive yet reasonably priced. Sessions at both schools are held four times every year. Every type of auction is covered in the curriculm at both schools and the staffs of both schools are proud of their assistance to graduates following graduation.

After school, you must then find the right site. Consider areas where flea markets are big business, but where auctioneers are not yet working. Consider, too, the social well-being of those who comprise your market. Ask yourself if your audiences can and will bid on a variety of items.

For example, those who attend an auction for medium priced household goods will not be the same as those who show up for expensive antiques, fine art or custom cars.

To locate property which will allow you to house goods, and hold a five hour auction which will not be affected by the weather, try to find a large building which has been vacant for awhile due to a failed business. Often, the owners of these types of buildings will listen to a proposal to accept a percentage of the profits as rent.

If the area where you go into business is heavily populated, chances are you can have several auctions each week which appeal to different audiences. On Monday, you might have an auction of Baseball Cards. On Wednesday, you may have an auction for Tools and Equipment. On Friday, you may have an auction on Recreational Vehicles and Trucks, etc.

Before reaching this point, however, you will need to do a lot of studying to know prices well. Only then can you quote percentage fees which will be acceptable to those bringing items on consignment and still allow you to profit.

When you run an ad, detail the times and categories so that buyers know when to attend and you don't waste their time.

At every auction, offer food at reasonable prices, even if it is simply doughnuts, hot dogs and soft drinks. Once you have established yourself in the community, then market your services through Real Estate agencies to handle Estate Sales. Once you hold an auction for wealthy clients and establish a track record for efficiency, your future will be even more promising.

Additional opportunities will come your way by finding closeout purchases which you can auction off and more than double your profit.

CONSIDER JOINING THIS ASSOCIATION

National Auctioneers Association
8880 Ballentine
Overland Park, KS 66214
Phone (913) 541-8084
(members receive Auctioneer Magazine)

PUBLICATIONS

Auction & Surplus
6730 San Fernando Road
Glendale, CA 91201
Phone (818) 240-5522

Art & Auction Magazine
250 W. 57th Street
New York, NY 10107
Phone (212) 582-5633

"Calm self-confidence is as far from conciet as the desire to earn a decent living is remote from greed."

Channing Pollock

AWNINGS

Here is another business which is one worth considering for those who have experience on a commercial sewing machine.

If you can afford to spend some time working at no pay, we suggest you go to awning companies and ask to work for nothing in return for knowledge and developing your skills.

Approach only those owners who are not in the area where you intend to go into business. Be honest with them. Say: "I intend to go into my own awning business in the (whatever city) area and I would like to work for you at no wage so I can learn the business."

If the owner says "no", count your blessings; he or she probably wouldn't help you much anyway. Keep looking for that owner who likes the idea of helping others. It is then you will be in the right spot.

In addition to awnings, also consider boat tops, convertible tops, truck covers, tents, and canopies.

To locate suppliers for canvas, visit your library and look up Canvas in the Thomas Register.

BALLOON GIFTS AND DECORATIONS

A fast growing alternative to giving fresh flowers for birthdays, anniversaries and other special events is a colorful balloon bouquet.

And what you deliver for $25.00 to $30.00 costs you only a couple of dollars with no risk of spoilage.

Using your imagination by having helium balloons pop out of boxes, by having a delivery person dressed as a clown, by having messages or dollars inside of balloons, by having balloons attached to gifts such as a kitten or puppy, by having helium balloons hold up a sign which says, "I love You", by having an entire trunk of a car loaded with helium balloons, etc.

Advertise in the local papers. Also sell a decorating service. You will decorate halls, malls, wedding cars, exhibition areas, picnic areas, whatever. You will prepare any location for a party, a convention, a wedding, a divorce, a grand opening, a bar-mitzvah or any other celebration.

Contact local businesses to inform them of your services in addition to running ads in the local papers as well as the yellow pages.

Contact all halls, and hotels and motels which have halls, which are rented out for special events.

Contact all Bridal Consultants. Tell them of your services.

At your first event be sure to take pictures to use to sell furniture clients.

You can have balloons made with client's names on them. You can release balloons with special store coupons in them.

You can have a special prize for the person who finds the balloon with the winning number in it. Of course the finder must come to the store to match the number on display. You can decorate store windows. You can actually make balloon sculptures.

Best of all you can make profits that are sensational.

Consider joining the **National Association of Balloon Artists,** P.O. Box 43472, Jacksonville, FL 32201. Phone (904) 388-9060. This association publishes a magazine titled *Balloon Today.*

To discuss this with a consultant, call

Balloon City, U.S.A.
1021 Market Street
Harrisburg, PA 00000
Phone (717) 939-1009.

BALLOON SUPPLIERS. Call or write them for catalogs.

Balloon Baron
1279 W. Stowell Road
Santa Maria, CA 93454
Phone 1-800-235-4112 or (805) 922-0564

Balloon Company Of America
18775-G N. Frederick Road
Gaithersburg, MD 20879
Phone 1-800-638-9581 or (301) 921-9444

U.S. Balloon Co.
140 58th Street, Brooklyn Army Terminal
Brooklyn, NY 11220
Phone 1-800-221-1665

Rodin Industries, Inc.
824 S. Washington Avenue
Scranton, PA 18505
Phone 1-800-366-7634

Dipcraft Manufacturing Co.
111 W. Braddock Avenue
Braddock, PA 15104
Phone 1-800-245-6145

Balloon Stuffing is another side of this business that offers additional ways to make money. It's a new concept for gift giving. You can deliver a bottle of champagne, a couple glasses, snacks and whatever, all in a large balloon tied with a colorful ribbon. You can even package teddy bears, dolls, toys, jewelry, plants and numerous other items in this unique way. The secret is in the ingenious equipment.

For more details and all the supplies you'll need, contact:

Pretty Balloon International
Plaza 1000, Main Street, Suite 600
Voorhees, NJ 08043
Phone (609) 627-9343

"Advertising is 85% confusion
and 15% commission."

Fred Allen

BOOK BAG, SHOPPING BAG, BACK PACK BUSINESS.

This business is easily started in the home, and there is no need for storage space as your entire business will be wholesale.

In addition to your sewing ability, however, you will need to master two other skills, selling and silk-screening.

Your customers will primarily be local schools, retail department stores, souvenir shops, sporting goods stores, resorts and hotel lobby shops.

Once you learn silk-screening, you can also branch out into custom T-shirts, sweat shirts, bumper stickers, posters, signs, binders and many other items.

If this is not a skill taught where you are now, consult your school sytems to find out if classes are available. If none are being offered, then again, go to an owner of a local silk-screen business and offer to work for very little, or even nothing, in return for learning the business. Be honest with the owner, telling him or her your recent history and of your intention to open your own business.

BRICKMASON, SELF EMPLOYED CONTRACTOR

If this type of work appeals to you, you can be the one in seven brickmasons who is self employed.

There is a lot of lifting in this trade so you should be in good shape. You also must be good at using plumblines and levels.

Brickmasons work with cinderblock as well as concrete blocks, bricks, stone and artificial stone.

To remain employed, you may have to travel to locations where building is going on.

To start in this trade after learning it, call on every general contractor within your county and every adjoining county. Ask for work while giving your assurance that you are honest, reliable, neat and efficient.

If you intend to relocate in another area of the country, be sure to call or write the Chamber of Commerce and general contractors to inquire about current construction.

If you don't know this trade but would like to learn, write the following schools for their catalog and tuition fees:

Greensburg Institute of Technology
302 West Otterman Street
Greensburg, PA 15601
Phone (412) 837-3330

Williamson Free School of Mechanical Trades
106 South New Middletown Road
Media, PA 19063
Phone (215) 566-1776

American Masonry Institute
5306 Washington Avenue
Houston, TX 77007
Phone (713) 229-8366

CONTACT THIS ORGANIZATON REGARD-
ING MEMBERSHIP AND BENEFITS:

**International Union Of Bricklayers & Allied
Craftsmen.**
815 15th Street, N.W.
Washington, D.C. 20005
Phone (202) 783-3788

Publish a monthly journal. 106,000 members.

"Let the past be buried,
except those memories
which serve as examples
which should never be
repetitious."

Arendee

CAKES FOR SPECIAL EVENTS

You can begin in your kitchen at home. The only items you need are a unique collection of pans which the average housewife doesn't have, the acquired skill of cake decorating, and love for baking.

Advertise in local papers and by all means get into the yellow pages as soon as possible. Other promotion ideas worth considering are: contacting all clubs, organizations, hotels, restaurants, major employers, etc. to let them know that you can deliver a great cake for less than a large bakery might charge.

Although you will be particularly busy preceding every holiday, you will have more than enough business every week of the year with birthdays, anniversaries, reunions, retirements, grand openings and weddings.

The key to longevity in this business is simple. Just produce a beautifully decorated cake which tastes as good as it looks. A baking schedule which allows you to deliver a fresh cake is a must. If you can't deliver it fresh, then turn down the business. Having a dependable reputation for quality will provide you with a substantial income even as you continually expand to larger quarters and increase your volume.

CONTACT THIS ORGANIZATION REGARDING MEMBERSHIP AND BENEFITS:

Retail Bakers of America
6525 Belcrest Rd., Presidential Bldg., Suite 250
Hyattsville, MD 20782
Phone (301) 907-3202

Publish numerous publications. 2925 members.

CARPENTER, SELF EMPLOYED CONTRACTOR

If being a carpenter sounds like work you would enjoy, it is not difficult to get work as a sub-contractor. It will be necessary, however, to move to locations where building is in full swing.

During economic slowdowns, you may have to depart from new construction to concentrate on the Home Repair Business, but for the most part you can stay in business if you gain a reputation for quality work.

If you work on new home construction you will have to decide whether you would care to specialize in rough carpentry or finished carpentry.

Once you are accomplished in this field, make personal calls on all general contractors in your county and all adjoining counties. Ask to bid on their next job. Also make a point of telling these individuals that you are honest, reliable, prompt and neat in addition to being efficient.

General contractors are pleased to work with sub-contractors who take pride in their work.

If you don't know carpentry now, but would like to learn, contact the schools listed below which you find of interest:

North Bennet Street School
39 North Bennet Street
Boston, MA 02113
Phone (617) 227-0155

School Of Trades
240 N. Franklintown Road
Baltimore, MD 21223
Phone (301) 566-7111

Ranken Technical Institute
4431 Finney Avenue
St. Louis, MO 63113
Phone (314) 371-0236

Greensburg Institute Of Technology
302 West Otterman Street
Greensburg, PA 15601
Phone (412) 837-3330

Johnson Technical Institute
3427 North Main Avenue
Scranton, PA 18508
Phone (717) 343-6404

Orleans Technical Institute
1330 Rhawn Street
Philadelphia, PA 19111
Phone (215) 728-4700

Triangle Tech
180 Exit 16, P.O. Box 551
DuBois, PA
Phone (814) 371-2090

Williamson Free School Of Mechanical Trades
106 South New Middletown Road
Media, PA 19063
Phone (215) 566-1776

New England Institute Of Technology
2500 Post Road
Warwick, RI 02886
Phone (401) 722-2003

CONTACT THIS ORGANIZATION RE-
GARDING MEMBERSHIP AND BENEFITS:

**United Brotherhood of Carpenters and Joiners
of America.**
101 Constitution Avenue, N.W.
Washington, D.C. 20001
Phone (202) 546-6206

Publish a monthly journal. 700,000 members.

**"Conformity is the treadmill
most of us are content to
walk. Great men blaze new
trails, where there is less
traffic, but more promise."**

Gary B. Wright

CARPET CLEANING

Although this is a highly competitive business, you can get started rather easily by offering to clean one room for a reduced amount to show customers the quality of your work.

You'll need a van that looks good, (even though it may be old), and commercial carpet cleaning equipment and supplies which could total a few thousand dollars.

According to those in the trade, entrepreneurs can average about $32.00 per hour for the time spent on the job. If you intend to give on-site estimates and calculate each job by the square foot, you must realize that you will have fewer hours when you are actually making money.

You may be better off quoting a price over the phone. Most people can give you a pretty good approximation of the size of their rooms. Take their word for it, rather than ask them to measure each area exactly. This may occasionally give your customer a real bargain, but you will save precious time. For commercial customers, always make a personal call.

Another "hand-in-hand" service that is worthwhile offering is upholstery cleaning. Equipment and chemicals for this work are generally available from the same sources from which you will be purchasing your carpet cleaning supplies.

One such supplier is the Von Schrader Co. in Wisconsin. We recommend them as they offer purchasers capable training, partial financing, and continuing problem-solving support.

EQUIPMENT AND CHEMICAL SUPPLIERS.

Call or write for catalogs:

Von Schrader Co.
1600 Junction Avenue
Racine, WI 53403
Phone (414) 634-1956

Zep Manufacturing Co.
Dept. S-10
1310-T Seaboard Industrial Blvd.
Atlanta, GA 30318
Phone (404) 355-3120

Hild Floor Machine Co.
5339 W. Lake Street
Chicago, IL 60644
Phone (312) 379-8558

ABSO Clean Industries
17325 Lamont Street
Detroit, MI 48212
Phone 1-800-837-5000

CITY TOUR OPERATOR

Visitors to every sizeable city in this country always want to know what there is to see and do. You can be the answer.

Put together full and half-day tours which include transportation to unique spots of interest.

You can make money by charging a specific fee for each member of the group you are escorting, and additional money from the owners of tourist attractions and restaurants who will pay you for bringing business their way.

Places of interest might include: manufacturing plants, cathedrals, zoos, homes of famous people living and dead, waterfalls, historic battle sites, museums, theaters, gardens, archaeological sites, nightclubs, amusement parks, ethnic areas of the city, unusual landscapes, haunted houses, etc.

Design a set patter to use and include as many jokes as you can. You want to be both informative and entertaining.

If you have enough money for a down payment on a van or an old bus, you're in business. If not, then sell the tour to a group, then lease a bus and driver.

After putting down several tours on paper, actually drive the route and get the timing down pat. Talk to restaurant owners about a kick-back, but don't take your group to a lousy restaurant just because the owner will give you a better percentage. Your reputation is important. Make sure the food is excellent.

After you have your tours down on paper, have them typeset and printed on a flyer you can leave at prominent motels, hotels, fraternal organizations, church groups, etc.

Keep in mind that your tours do not have to be by van or bus. Boats, airplanes, gliders, hot air balloons, bicycles, rafts, horses, camels, wagons, or any combination of the above is great.

The more exciting and unusual your tours can be, the faster your reputation will grow.

Not only can you have a lot of fun with this business, but you can make a very handsome income.

If business is slow to start, advertise your services in the local paper.

In addition to tours, organize hayrides, treasure hunts, rallys, nature hikes, safaris, pilgrimages, etc. Use your imagination.

The bottom line is this: people will pay well to be entertained and experience something different in their lives.

If you have a good imagination, like the idea of entertaining and are willing to work hard, this could be the business for you.

Choose the city you would like to live in. Get out the yellow pages and start calling. After you have complete details on everything in town, and whatever fees are changed, calculate what you must charge so that you make an excellent wage.

As your business grows, you can start hiring others who will work as independent agents. You can have any number of associates without the necessity of hiring full time employees.

CHIMNEY CLEANING

This business is worth considering for two very good reasons. You can make extraordinary earnings of more than $50.00 per hour, and you will have a business with few competitors.

Now you will need about $3,000.00 to get started, but this very modest investment includes your equipment, training, newsletters and some excellent marketing advice.

Nearly 100 million homes, factories and businesses have flues, stoves and chimneys which should be cleaned annually to prevent the possibility of disastrous fires.

For more information call or write to:

Austin West Systems
38 Austin Street
Box 658
Worcester, MA 01601
1-800-225-4016

COLD SANDWICH AND COLD DRINK CATERING WITHOUT A TRUCK.

If you are really working on a shoestring, here is a business you can start with just a few dollars. You can make sandwiches, cookies and other baked goods at home, load them carefully into a large wicker basket, and then take them to office buildings to sell.

Before starting this business, you need to check two things: whether your city, or township requires you to have a license for such a business and whether a health card is required to be a food handler.

After getting approval, you then start going to large office buildings to ask for permission to solicit the tenants. This may be easier for you if you offer the person in charge 10% of the profits. If this is necessary, simply adjust your prices so you can make the profit you have in mind.

If you are not sure what to charge, visit all the restaurants near the buildings you will be serving and note their prices. As far as drinks go, just carry a few cans inside your basket in an insulated ice bag. Trying to guess what to carry will become easier as you learn the particular likes of your customers. Whenever possible, take orders for the next day.

If your basket is difficult to carry, consider getting a skateboard to set it on as you push it around corridors.

Another innovation you might consider is wearing an unusual costume, perhaps as some character out of history or a nursery rhyme, or even just as a clown. If both you and the costume are colorful, and cheerful, people will look forward to seeing you each day.

CONTACT THIS ORGANIZATION REGARD-
ING MEMBERSHIP AND BENEFITS:

International Caterers Association
220 South State Street, Suite 1416
Chicago, IL 60604
Phone (312) 922-0966

Publish numerous publications. 3000 members.

"Nothing astonishes men
so much as
common sense and
plain dealing."

Ralph Waldo Emerson

COMPUTER REPAIR SERVICE

After going to school to learn to be a Computer Service Technician, you can easily start your own business.

Your yellow pages ad will bring you a steady flow of calls, but building this business depends on signing clients to annual service contracts.

Going door to door in office buildings for a few days will usually pay off well, as you will be competing in price with large companies with costly overheads.

If you are geographically close to computer parts warehouses, you will need little inventory to start. On the other hand, if you are starting in a small town, away from suppliers, you may find it difficult to compete with big guys.

If you have already learned this trade, consider joining one or both of these Industry Associations:

National Computer Service Network
90 Crossways Park Drive
Woodbury, NY 11797
Phone (516) 682-5300

United Service Network
3540 Tilden
Orange, CA 92669
Phone (714) 639-1162

PUBLICATION

Electronic Servicing & Technology
P.O. Box 12901
Overland Park, KS 66212
Phone (913) 888-4664

TO LOCATE A SCHOOL WHICH TEACHES
COMPUTER REPAIR, CONTACT:

**The National Association of Trade And
Technical Schools**
2251 Wisconsin Avenue, N.W.
Washington, D.C. 20007
Phone (202) 333-1021

CONTACT THIS ORGANIZATION REGARD-
ING MEMBERSHIP AND BENEFITS:

**North American Computer Service
Association**
100 Silver Beach, #918
Daytona Beach, FL 32118
Phone (904) 255-9040

"Difficulties strengthen the mind, as labor does the body."

Seneca

COURT REPORTING

If you consider yourself a good typist, being a Court Reporter is a super occupation for a person who wants to be his/her own boss. The hourly rate of pay is considerably above average and you can freelance your services.

There are many schools which offer training in this career, but often the courses are titled, "Shorthand Reporter."

Contact the following School Organizations for their directories. They will be sent at no cost. You will find schools which offer this training in every area of this country.

The National Association of Trade and Technical Schools
2251 Wisconsin Avenue, N.W.
Washington, D.C. 20007
Phone (202) 333-1021

Association of Independent Colleges and Schools
One Dupont Circle, N.W., Suite 350
Washington, D.C. 20036
Phone (202) 659-2460

CONTACT THIS ORGANIZATION REGARDING MEMBERSHIP AND BENEFITS:

National Shorthand Reporters Association
118 Park Street, S.E.
Vienna, VA 22180
Phone (703) 281-4677

Publish many publications. 26,000 members.

CUSTOM CAR CLEANING WHILE YOUR CUSTOMERS ARE AT WORK.

This is another business you can start with just a few dollars, but if you have an ample supply of elbow grease it won't be long before you have a sensational income.

Here is the concept. Go to the parking garages in major downtown cities. Ask to speak to the owner or the person in charge. Propose that you wash and clean cars in the spaces where they are parked. For allowing you to do that you will give this person 10% of your gross income. When they agree, you then tell them that you will also need their permission to put sales flyers under the windshield wipers of all the cars which park there every day under contract. Your customers call you at home. When you finish a job, you leave a bill under the windshield along with a stamped self-addressed envelope.

Water is available at all these buildings. You simply need to buy yourself cleaning and waxing supplies, a Shop-Vac, and some account books to keep accurate records.

If you have more business than you can handle as the result of making agreements with many garages, then hire some workers. Consult an attorney about hiring people as casual labor, rather than putting individuals on the payroll as employees.

One more item is essential if there is no one at your home to answer the phone at all times. That, of course, is an answering machine. There are some good ones available now for less than $100.00.

DOORSCOPE SALES & INSTALLATION

This item is brand new, and offers anyone who can talk and operate a hand drill a sensational self-employment opportunity.

The Doorscope is a well made High Tech optical instrument which can be installed in minutes in any door.

It allows a person to stand up to 7 feet away from a door and get a camera's eye view of the other side. A wide angle lens presents a clear picture which even a child can see from well below the unit.

This is one of those items that sells itself. Once seen, few prospects will say no, as it is obvious that once installed, inhabitants will feel more secure.

You can start your own business by simply buying these units for around $30.00 and selling them for $69.00 or $89.00 installed. Contact:

Burton Products, Inc.
3701-A West Cypress
Tampa, FL 33679
In Florida, call 1-813-872-6276
Others call: 1-800-365-7267

DOWNTOWN LUNCH DELIVERY BUSINESS

This idea may cost a few thousand dollars to put into effect, but far, far less than it would cost to open sit-down restaurant. The reason? You can rent space anywhere, even in the basement of an office building as long as it is near high-rise buildings. You will not be dealing with walk-in trade.

Here's the concept. You distribute an attractive luncheon menu and check-off luncheon order forms to all offices in high-rise buildings. You also provide instructions to check off the items wanted for lunch, any special directions for preparation, the time the lunch is to be delivered, and a request to Fax the order to you two hours prior to the time of requested delivery.

You have young boys and girls lined up to make the deliveries. With minimum wage plus tips, this should be a very desirable job.

As business increases, you continually add more Fax machines. As the business grows, consider uniforms for your delivery kids. Your Fax-phone number should appear on the back of every uniform. Also worth considering is a discount for orders Faxed a day a head of time. As you are doing your marketing, also let it be known that you cater to office parties, providing cakes, balloons, entertainment, costumed delivery people who sing, etc.

Vitally important: don't allow any delivery people to start before you thoroughly train them in courtesy, what to do and say, and what not to do and say, how to smile, how to apologize even though you know you're not wrong, how to make change, and if necessary, how to write a credit card charge. All delivery people should also know that because most orders are going to be requested around the same time, that hustling is absolutely essential. Those who take too much time must be promptly replaced.

This business has tremendous potential as many downtown workers can't easily get to their cars to drive somewhere for lunch. Others don't like going out as it takes too long, and often it means waiting in line. Sending a secretary out to pick up something is also expensive.

As long as you concentrate on top quality food and prompt, responsible service, you could be well on your way to a very prosperous future. Another advantage to this type of food service is that generally you can work far fewer hours than those required at a sit-down restaurant. You will be dealing with breakfast and lunch only, unless you are catering an event which takes place later in the day.

> ## "Experience is a hard teacher because she gives the test first, the lesson afterwards."
>
> **Vernon Sanders Law**

ESTATE SALE ORGANIZER (GARAGE SALE)

There are many people, who when moving, do not have the time or inclination to run a garage sale. But as always, they have many things they don't care to drag along to their new location which are too good to throw out.

This is where you come in. For 25% to 40% of gross sales, you go to the client's home and schedule the sale, asking the owners to leave during the hours of the sale.

You price all items with tags and make a complete inventory list on paper so you can have accurate records for yourself and the owner.

You then advertise in the classified columns of local newspapers. Once people attend a sale which you have organized, your reputation will grow, if you have done a good job, and subsequent sales will draw more people.

It is a good idea to have someone assist you at the sale if for no other reason than to make sure items aren't stolen.

To promote your new business, start by calling on all real estate firms in your area. Leave printed flyers which can be given to those who have just sold their homes.

As your business grows, have ads in the yellow pages and the local press. Time allowing, call all the real estate ads in the classified section which have been placed by homeowners who are selling their own homes. Just get their names and addresses and send them a flyer if they indicate an interest in your service.

When you first call on a client, you must explain to them that an item in "like new" condition can at best be sold for 50% of the original cost. Items that show wear must be sold for less. This must be made clear to begin with, as many people feel their belongings are worth far more than they really are.

People who attend garage sales, or to be more dignified, "estate sales", are bargain hunters. Pricing items too high will produce few sales, and kill your reputation. Your clients must understand this. If they contest every item you price, then turn down the job.

To promote a professional reputation, have the name of your company on every price tag. Have signs about the size of real estate signs with your company name on them for placement on neighboring streets. These are to direct people to the location of the sale and tell readers of the date and time. The day before the sale starts, hire a youngster in the neighborhood to deliver flyers to all residences within a reasonable area. These notices must be professionally typeset and printed, not handwritten and run off on a copy machine. Again, let us stress your image as a professional.

Your appearance is also vitally important. Wearing suits, ties and dresses is wise. As they say in the commericals for Head & Shoulders shampoo, "you never get a second chance to make a first impression."

One last bit of advice. Don't accept for sale any appliances that don't work, any clothes that are ripped, torn, or simply worn out, any furniture that is not in reasonably good condition. In other words, let it be known that your company does not sell junk.

Your goal is to continue to sell your services to a wealthier clientele. Once you begin to get referrals from those in prominence, you have an opportunity to make an extraordinary income.

FLAG MANUFACTURING AND SALES

If you know how to operate a commercial sewing machine, you can start this business anywhere in a relatively small area.

Patriotism sells flags. With spirit running high in the United States as well as many other countries throughout the world, the market for flags is at an all time high.

You can start your flag business by running small ads in local newspapers, including ethnic periodicals, and calling on various nationality groups.

After sales get going, you can consider opening a Flag Store, perhaps a Flag and Map Store. As many national boundaries are not what they used to be, maps are needed and desired. As sources for maps and flags are few and far between, chances are you will have no competition.

National flags are certainly not all that are in demand. Banners, pennants and flags for organizations, schools, corporations, golf courses, funeral homes, boats, stadiums, professional and amateur sport teams, shopping malls, etc.

State flags are also becoming much more popular than ever before. Many retired seniors in Florida, Arizona, Texas and California have picked up on a unique practice. Any time they have guests from out-of-state, they hang out the flag from the state where their guests are from.

This brings up another way to profit: selling flag poles and the rigging to go with them.

If you can visualize yourself in this business and are excited about it, then start collecting pictures of maps and consult the Thomas Register in your library for the names of fabric manufacturers where you can purchase your materials.

You can start in this business for the cost of your machine and your initial order of cloth and thread. Few opportunities with so little risk . . . offer such great potential.

Now if you want to order flags already made and concentrate on sales, there are 18 pages of listings in the Thomas Register, Volume 5, which you might contact.

Our research indicates that the following companies have a record of quality and service:

Humphrys Flag Co., Inc.
238 Arch Street
Philadelphia, PA
In PA phone (215) 922-0510
Others 1-800-227-3524

Eder Manufacturing Co.
(have an 84 page catalog)
1000 West Rawson Ave
Oak Creek, WI 53154
In WI phone 1-800-472-5727
Others 1-800-558-6044

Atlas Flags
2010 Weems Road
Tucker, GA 30084
In GA call (404) 938-0003
Others 1-800-999-FLAG

Flags International
10845 McKinley Highway
Osceola, Indiana 46561
In IN phone (219) 674-5125
Others 1-800-627-3524

Valley Forge Corp.
935 Northern Boulevard
Great Neck, NY 10021
In NY phone: 1-800-US FLAGS
Others 1-800-847-4155

Metro Flag, Inc.
47 Bassett Highway
Dover, NJ 07801
Phone 1-800-666-FLAG

> *"Fortune knocks at every man's door once in life, but in a good many cases the man is in a neighboring saloon and does not hear her."*
>
> **Mark Twain**

GIFT BASKETS

This can be an excellent business, particularly around Christmas, as gift baskets are one of the few gifts you can send to everyone and generally the recipients will appreciate receiving them.

All you need is a source of excellent fruits, nuts, candies, non-perishable meats, wines, cheeses or whatever, some paper grass, some cellophane, some ribbons and some wicker baskets.

Call on hotels and motels. Let them know you can make up excellent baskets for V.I.P. guests.

Call on major employers. Let them know you can make up great baskets for their V.I.P. customers.

If businesses in your city manufacture or produce unique products which aren't available elsewhere, put together a special "Boston Gift Basket" or "San Francisco Gift Basket" or whatever. Then market them through gift shops in major hotels, at the airport, at tourist attractions, etc.

If this sounds like something you would enjoy doing, call or write for pictures of baskets you might use. Contact:

Oriental Horizons Inc.
48 East Main Street
Ramsey, NJ, 07446
Phone 1-201-327-0731

If you are able to buy in quantity, they will manufacture to your specifications at their plant in China. For smaller quantities they will set you up with a supplier in this country.

HOUSING INSPECTOR, RESIDENTIAL

This is a recession-proof business that you can start for less than a few hundred dollars. If you are familiar with residential construction, this business is right up your alley.

Buyers of used homes want no surprises after they move in. That's why more and more people are willing to hire an expert to inspect a house before signing a contract.

Nationwide, these inspectors now average over $1,000.00 per week in net income.

You can learn every aspect of this business without going to a resident school. An audio cassette course is available to you which makes learning easy. Additional checklists are included, as is information on marketing your services.

You are not restricted to dealing with home buyers. Banks, Savings & Loan Associations, Corporations and Real Estate companies will often use the services of a Housing Inspector.

Now here is the best part. This course is purchased for less than $100.00

Contact:

Test Institute
1110 Navaho Drive
Raleigh, NC 27612
Phone 1-800-868-7246

This course was designed by a Professional Architectural Co.

LANDSCAPING

If you like outside physical work in a variety of settings, this is a worthwhile business to consider.

It is also a business that is easy to start in any area of this country.

If you intend to stay up north, it is wise to consider snow removal in the winter to sustain an income.

If you intend to locate in the south, it is a good idea to know insect control and lawn diseases. The more you know, the more there will be a demand for your services.

You can start this business with no money whatsoever by soliciting lawn cutting jobs where you use the equipment of the owners. To get customers, simply offer a price that is considerably lower than established local competitors.

Make a commitment to yourself to save a certain percentage of every day's receipts so you can purchase your own equipment.

Your growth will thereafter be the result of your own effort.

In addition to maintaining the lots of home-owners, it is a good idea to pursue maintenance contracts with commercial accounts.

Other sources of excellent income for land-scapers: growing your own plants, shrubs, trees and even sod. Harvesting rocks for landscaping. Constructing recirculating fountains. Drawing landscape plans. Constructing bird feeders. Knowing methods of keeping animals from feeding on vegetation.

To prepare yourself well, check with your local community colleges to learn of all courses which may be of benefit. Attend whenever possible.

OTHER SOURCES OF INFORMATION

American Association of Nurserymen
1250 I Street, N.W., Suite 500
Washington, D.C. 20005
Phone (202) 789-2900

American Society of Landscape Architects
1733 Connecticut Avenue, N.W.
Washington, D.C. 20009
Phone (202) 466-7730

PUBLICATIONS:

American Nurseryman
111 N. Canal Street
Chicago, IL 60606
Phone (312) 782-5505

Garden Supply Retailer
P.O. Box 2400
Minneapolis, MN 55343
Phone (612) 931-0211

Nursery Business
Northwood Plaza Station
Clearwater, FL 33519
Phone (813) 796-3877

LOCKSMITHING

You won't get rich in this business, but you can certainly gain above-average earnings.

Once you have learned this trade, have some calling cards made and hit the road. Call on every hotel, motel, apartment house, hospital, resort, school, train station, bus station, airport, office building, etc. in your area. Tell them you are honest, reliable, punctual and efficient. Ask for their business.

If you keep asking, you will get enough business to immediately pay your bills, particularly if you are working out of your home. Paying rent for a retail business is simply not smart to start off with. This is not a business where you will have a lot of walk-in trade.

After getting started, you can branch out into security devices and alarm systems.

The tools necessary to start are not costly. Even with a grinder and key-making machine, you can start for less than $1000.00.

The following locksmithing schools offer resident classes in locksmithing. Contact them to request their school catalog.

Omni College
7636 Burnet Avenue
Van Nuys, CA 91405
Phone (818) 787-6664

North Bennet Street School
39 North Bennet Street
Boston, MA 02113
Phone (617) 227-0155

National School of Locksmithing & Alarms
1466 Broadway, 2nd Floor
New York, NY 10036
Phone (800) 223-6466

This trade can also be learned through home study courses. If you have the self-discipline to study on your own, then consider contacting the following school to request more information:

McGraw-Hill Continuing Education Center (NRI Schools)
4401 Connecticut Avenue, N.W.
Washington, D.C. 20008

CONTACT THIS ORGANIZATION REGARDING MEMBERSHIP AND BENEFITS:

Associated Locksmiths of America
3003 Live Oak Street
Dallas, TX 75204
Phone (214) 827-1701

Publish many publications. 7000 members.

MOBILE OIL AND LUBE SERVICE

With the decline of the full service gas station, new business opportunities have emerged, not the least of which is the quick lubrication industry.

From coast to coast, these centers have been popping up and for the most part they have been successful.

It is possible, however, to service as many customers with a mobile van and avoid the costly expense of renting or constructing a building.

Customers who have difficulty finding the time to go to one of these centers will particularly appreciate the fact that you can come to where their car is parked.

Average charge these days is approximately $22.00 for an oil change and a lube job. As your supply cost for oil, filter, and windshield wiper fluid will be $17.00. The average time used to complete each job is 15 minutes; consequently there is great profit potential here if you can schedule numerous appointments without spending a lot of time on the road.

We suggest you try to line up customers who own fleets of trucks, cars or vans.

You'll need enough money to outfit a van with a hydraulic jack, tanks for waste oil, a water tank, a generator which will allow you to check the air pressure in tires, an air hose, lube guns, a gauge to check anti-freeze, etc.

If you are able to finance the truck, chances are you can be in business for less than $2000.00

To gain customers who will be steady customers, we suggest you call first on potential business clients who have multiple vehicles. Office buildings, large real estate firms, medical facilities, contractors, etc. are also types of businesses which allow you to service many clients without moving your truck.

Additional profits can be made by selling wiper blades, hoses, belts, air filters, head lights, tail lights, batteries, and by selling the waste oil you collect.

Now, if you can come up with more money, you may be interested in contacting a company which has already analyzed this business thoroughly and designed a completely equipped van. They also offer their clients the benefits of their experience, training, and assistance with bookkeeping systems, billing, and other record keeping.

As we always advocate learning from the experience of others, we urge you to call:

Oil Can Van, Inc.
One Flagler Avenue
Stuart, Florida 34994.
Phone 1-800-545-9626

"Shallow men believe in luck. Strong men believe in cause and effect."

Ralph Waldo Emerson

MASSAGE THERAPIST

This career is seldom considered as one for those who would prefer to be self-emloyed, but we feel it is a good one.

You will have to go to school for some 500 to 700 hours, and be certified by the state where you intend to work, but your effort will be rewarded.

You can contract your services with local hospitals and clinics, and/or establish a portable business where you give massages to wealthy clients by appointment.

If this sounds interesting to you, contact the following schools and request their catalog:

Desert Institute of the Healing Arts
639 North Sixth Avenue
Tucson, AZ 85705
Phone (602) 882-0899

Connecticut Center for Massage Therapy
75 Kitts Lane
Newington, CT 06111
Phone (203) 667-1886

Suncoast School of Massage Therapy
4910 Cypress Street
Tampa, FL 33607
Phone (813) 287-1099

The Humanities Center School of Massage
3565 Cypress Terrace
Pinellas Park, FL 34665
Phone (813) 522-1697

Atlanta School of Massage
2300 Peachford Road, Suite 3200
Atlanta, GA 30338
Phone (404) 454-7167

Bancroft School of Massage Therapy
50 Franklin Street
Worcester, MA 01608
Phone (508) 757-7923

The Swedish Institute
226 West 26th Street, 5th Floor
New York, NY 10001
Phone (212) 924-5900

CONTACT THIS ORGANIZATION REGARD-
ING MEMBERSHIP AND BENEFITS:

**Associated Professional Massage Therapists
And Bodyworkers**
1746 Cole Boulevard, Suite 225
Golden, CO 80401
Phone (303) 674-8478

2000 members.

*"The man who makes no
mistakes does not usually
make anything."*

Edward Phelps

PAINTING HOUSES AND COMMERCIAL BUILDINGS

Despite the fact that we all think we know how to paint, there is a great deal more to this profession than the average person thinks there is.

You must know what goes over what, types of paints, varnishes, fillers, how to mix, how to match, types of brushes, strokes, spraying, available equipment, etc.

Also less evident than the average person thinks is the money that can be made in this business if you have the latest equipment and aren't afraid to work.

At any given time, in any area of this country, there are painting jobs to be done.

Most of the time, all it will take for you to get started is a small classified ad in the local paper or a well done advertising flyer delivered door to door. If you like the idea of using an ad flyer, please spend a few more dollars to have it typeset and printed by professionals. If you distribute a sloppy ad, people will assume your work as a painter will also be sloppy.

IF YOU WOULD LIKE TO TAKE A CLASS IN PAINTING, CONSIDER:

Williamson Free School of Mechanical Trades
106 South New Middletown Road
Media, PA 19063
Phone (215) 566-1776

This school also teaches paperhanging, which is an excellent skill for a painter to have as it is a source of higher hourly earnings than painting demands.

TO GET A CATALOG OF PAINTING EQUIP-
MENT AND SUPPLIES, CONTACT:

Dynacraft Industries
299 Greenwood Road
Morganville, NJ 07791
Phone 1-800-922-0621

Now unless you live in Pennsylvania, it will probably be difficult for you to get to the Williamson
School. So just go down to your local painting supply
house and start asking questions. You could even ask
to work for someone for a week or so at no wage in
return for training.

CONTACT THIS ORGANIZATION REGARD-
ING MEMBERSHIP AND BENEFITS:

**International Brotherhood of Painters &
Allied Trades.**
United Unions Building
1750 New York Avenue, N.W.
Washington, D.C. 20006
Phone (202) 637-0720

Publish a monthly journal. 162,295 members.

PAINTING PARKING LOT LINES.

You can be in this business for a very small investment, the price of a pole, a roller, a pan and some paint. After a few sales, however, you can quickly advance to bidding on larger jobs by buying the equipment necessary to do jobs more professionally and with greater speed.

If this sounds interesting to you, then call or write:

Dynacraft Industries
299-T Greenwood Road
Morganville, NJ 07791
Phone 1-800-922-0621, extension 22

Ask for their free catalog. They carry a complete line of painting equipment, accessories, and supplies.

Acquaint yourself with the equipment so that you can begin to visualize yourself in this business.

> **"A man can fail many times, but he isn't a failure until he begins to blame somebody else."**
>
> **John Burroughs**

PET CARE, GROOMING, HOUSING, TRAINING

If you like animals, more specifically dogs and cats, there is a great deal of money to be made in this business. Now you will have to invest in the tuition at a reputable Dog Grooming School to learn your trade, but thereafter you can start in business with a used van as your mobile office.

As business picks up you can go on to have your own multi-service business including a Pet Motel and a Pet Boutique.

If this sounds interesting, write or call:

The National Association of Trade & Technical Schools
2251 Wisconsin Avenue, N.W.
Washington, D.C. 20007
Phone (202) 333-1021

Ask for their directory of schools. It will be sent to you at no cost.

Courses are available in a number of states to become an animal trainer or a pet groomer.

PIANO TUNING

As long as you are not tone deaf, here's an opportunity for self-employment which is just plain fun for the musically inclined.

And suprisingly, you can make an excellent income as you most probably won't have too many competitors.

If you like this idea, but don't have any idea how to proceed, consider taking a home-study course. Contact:

Randy Potter School of Piano Technology
61592 Orion Drive
Bend, Oregon 97702
Phone (505) 382-5411

If you would prefer to go to a resident school, contact one or more of the following schools for information:

Special Talladega Technical Facility
(For the visually handicapped)
P.O. Box Drawer 17
Talladega, AL 35160

American Institute of Piano Technology
P.O. Box 4418
Chatsworth, CA 91311
Phone (213) 223-2010

Niles Bryant School of Piano Tuning
Dept. G
P.O. Box 19700
Sacramento, CA 95819
Phone (916) 454-4748

San Francisco School of Piano Tuning
657 Mission Street
San Francisco, CA 94105
Phone (415) 824-TUNE

Larry Crabb Piano Tuning & Technology
4299 Hugh Howell Road
Atlanta, GA 30084
Phone (404) 491-1432

Western Iowa Tech
P.O. Box 265
Sioux City, IA 51102
Phone (712) 274-6400

New England Conservatory of Music
P.O. Box 8307, Kennedy Station
Boston, MA 02115
Phone (617) 262-1120, ext. 365

North Bennet Street School
39 North Bennet Street
Boston, MA 02113
Phone (617) 227-0155

Michigan State University
Professor Owen Jorgensen
East Lansing, MI 48824
Phone (517) 353-0684

Edward W. Graf
13 Anette Park Drive
Bozeman, MT 59712
Phone (406) 586-9149

Museum Of The American Piano
211 W. 58th Street
New York, NY 10019
Phone (212) 246-4646

Steinway & Sons, Gary Green
Steinway Place
Long Island City, NY 11105
Phone (718) 721-2600

Central Piedmont Community College
P.O. Box 35009
Charlotte, NC 28235

Perkins School of Piano Tuning & Tech
225 Court Street
Elyria, OH 44035
Phone (216) 323-1440

The Piano Shoppe, Inc.
6825 Germantown Avenue
Philadelphia, PA 19119
Phone (215) 438-7038

Grayson County College
6101 Grayson Drive
Denison, TX 75020
Phone (214) 465-6030

Houston Community College
5514 Clara
Houston, TX 77041
Phone (713) 466- 6654

Shenandoah College & Conservatory
1460 College Drive
Winchester, VA 22601
Phone (703) 665-4581

**The Emil Fries Piano Hospital &
Training Center
(For the visually handicapped)**
2501 E. Evergreen Blvd.
Vancouver, WA 98661

West Virginia School For The Blind
Romney, WV 26757

IF YOU ARE INTERESTED IN THIS TRADE,
JOINING THIS ASSOCIATION IS A MUST:

Piano Technicians Guild
4510 Belleview, Suite 100
Kansas City, MO 64111
Phone (816) 753-7747

They'll be glad to send you information on membership, their publication, annual meetings and conventions.

"If there be any truer measure of a man than by what he does, it must be by what he gives."

Robert South

POOL CLEANING

Another business that you can start for a few dollars and expand rapidly. Locating in an area where folks have both pools and sizeable incomes is a must.

To begin, we suggest that you survey one neighborhood at a time, recording the addresses of all homes with pools. Then send a letter offering your services for less money than the established services in the area which have the overhead of a store.

Once you have established a route for every day of the week, you can begin to save towards buying a new truck, then owning your own building and hiring employees.

For a catalog listing a complete line of swimming pool supplies, chemicals and equipment write:

Bel Aqua
748 Main Street
New Rochelle, NY 10805
In NY phone 1-914-235-2200
Others 1-800-344-7946.

REAL ESTATE APPRAISING

Although laws governing real estate appraising will vary from state to state, this is one of those rare businesses which you can start as an individual and make earnings in excess of $100,000.00 per year without hiring employees and while working out of your home.

Once you have shown local banks and lending institutions that your work is professional, prompt and thorough, you will have it made.

Now you will have to learn how to be an appraiser but this can be done via correspondence.

Call or write for a free Career Booklet:

National College of Appraisal
2245 Perimeter Park
Atlanta, GA 30341.
1-800-223-4542

Before signing up for any course, however, we suggest you visit some bank mortgage departments and/or some mortgage brokers and ask them this question: if my new appraisal company offered to perform ten appraisals for you at no charge, would you take us up on our offer? Their answers should reveal if you have any potential business in the area in which you intend to locate.

CONTACT THIS ORGANIZATION REGARD-ING MEMBERSHIP AND BENEFITS:

American Institute Of Real Estate Appraisers
430 N. Michigan Avenue
Chicago, IL 60611-4088
Phone (312) 329-8559
6909 members.

RECYCLING BROKER OR CONSULTANT

When choosing a business to enter, it is a good idea to look down the road a few years to see what the experts believe will happen in the future.

When you do this with this business, you see nothing but greater opportunity and enormous profits.

At the present time, the Environmental Protection Agency (EPA) estimates that each person in this country generates 3.6 pounds of waste.

As you can see, at this rate areas to bury these mountains of trash are becoming harder to find. The answer is to recycle much of this collection, but at the present time only 15% is recycled.

If you see yourself as a good negotiator, this national problem can directly lead to your new business.

Cities, counties, municipalities, and corporations want answers as to how they can participate in a recycling program. As a consultant, you step in for a fee and set up a plan. You also arrange for contracts between collectors and those plants who actually recycle paper, or plastic, or aluminum, or other metals.

As a broker, you actually set up and negotiate contracts rather than just bringing the principals together. You make a complete study of all those who will purchase specific waste products. You then market your services to corporations, communities, etc.

The EPA has set a goal to further reduce generated waste by 25%. This will create many opportunities for brokers and consultants.

To get started, send $69.50 to:

Entrepreneur Group
2392 Morse Avenue
P.O. Box 19787
Irvine, CA 92713-9438
1-800-421-2300

Ask for Business Guide No. E1351, "Recycling Constultant/Broker."

CALL THIS COMPANY TO ACQUAINT YOURSELF WITH THEIR SERVICES.

REI Distributors, Inc.
P.O. Box 5250
Somerset, N.J. 08875-5250
Phone (201) 271-1355

They design, construct, and operate Materials Recovery Facilities.

NATIONAL ASSOCIATIONS YOU SHOULD CONSIDER JOINING.

Institute of Scrap Recycling Industries
1627 K Street, N.W., Suite 700
Washington, D.C. 20006
Phone (202) 466-4050

This organization publishes a very informative magazine titled, *Scrap Processing & Recycling Magazine.*

National Recycling Coalition
1101 30th Street, N.W.
Washington, D.C. 20007
Phone (202) 625-6406

RECYCLING OLD TIRES

This is certainly one of the most fascinating opportunities we have come across and we recommend it to you without any reservations.

For the ridiculous sum of $28.00 you can purchase the complete know-how on a business which takes old tires and turns them into beautiful, durable, professional looking rubber mats.

What makes this business even more fascinating is that there are many garages, tire companies, gas stations, etc., which will actually pay you to take the old tires away. Land fills in many areas now charge $2.00 a tire to these dealers, so they are anxious to pay you up to that amount to haul them away.

This gets even better. The man who developed this business and all the machines involved really goes to extremes to give you your money's worth. In addition to exact plans to make all your machines, his materials include assembly directions, proven marketing and promotion ideas and a whole lot of horse sense which he picked up while building his business. His name is Ken Winan. Although he has made a fortune with his enterprise, he really enjoys helping others to start their own business.

Although our praise seems somewhat overwhelming, we think is is earned. Seldom in our research have we felt the sincerity and dedication to customers that we have felt while examining this offering.

If you like hands-on work and don't mind talking to folks, we think you'll love this business. Send a check made out to Ken Winan to: Owen Publishing Co., Battle Ground, WA 98604-0010. If you have questions, call (206) 887-8646.

Incidentally, you can assemble all the machinery and equipment you will need for this enterprise for less than $1,000.00 With any effort at all, you should be able to get back your investment and more within the first month of operation.

You risk nothing. If for any reason you don't like the materials you will receive, you can return them for a full refund.

> ## "Defeat is not the worst of failures. Not to have tried is the true failure."
>
> **George Edward Woodbury**

TEMPORARY EMPLOYMENT SERVICES

This is a business that can lead to extraordinary wealth and yet your work is all clerical.

You advertise for individuals who want to work and are available to work on a temporary basis.

Let's give you an example. A contractor I know had many men with different construction skills call him every day asking if any work was available. Most of the time he simply said no and hung up. Then one day it dawned on him that, although he couldn't use these men on a given day, maybe someone else could.

He started signing up the callers and kept lists. He also contacted all the contractors he knew and then those he didn't know, telling them to call when they needed temporary workers.

The last time I heard about him, he referred an average of 95 workers a day who worked at least 8 hours. In other words, he was making $1520.00 per day from this service and this wasn't his major job. He had to put in a few phones and hire a couple of employees to handle the calls and bill employers, but still made well over $1000.00 per day.

You can have different pools of people to serve different types of employers.

Groups worth considering include: secretarial, computer operators, court reporters, medical assistants, dental assistants, maids, babysitters, receptionists, models and legal assistants.

Another idea worth considering is running a service for older workers who, although retired, would like to work a few days a week. There are many employers who recognize the fact that older workers are usually more conscientious, are seldom late or absent, are honest and have better communication skills.

For further information consider joining the

National Association of Temporary Services
119 S. Saint Aspah Street
Alexandria, VA 22314
Phone (703) 549- 6287

"No race can prosper till it learns that there is as much dignity in tilling a field as in writing a poem."

Booker T. Washington

TAXI CAB OWNER AND OPERATOR

If you like to drive and have enough money to get a decent looking car, you can be in your own business soon.

Both cab lights for the roof of your car and the meter can be purchased from the same company. Write or call them to receive their catalog:

Cabometer, Inc.
528 South Wilmer Avenue
Anniston, AL 36202
Phone (205) 237-6771

The cost of the lights range from $19.00 to $98.00. The meter will cost you around $380.00.

As far as being licensed to own and drive a cab, contact your city or county officials. You will also have to obtain a chauffeur's license and have sufficient insurance as required by your state laws.

All things considered, however, it is possible to start in this business for less than $1000.00 if you are able to finance the car and pay a partial amount of the insurance.

Once started, make sure that no less than 10% of all your earnings is banked so that you can move up to better equipment when sufficient funds are available.

Another aspect of this business to consider is having your own portable phone. Makes it easier to gain steady customers.

UPHOLSTERING

If you like the idea of repairing upholstered furniture and you have an area at home large enough to work, this is an excellent business. Not only can you make a fine income, but you can do so in good times and bad.

You'll need a truck, fabric samples, a mallet, hammers, chisels, tack pullers and sewing equipment, but all in all you can start with less than $2000.00.

Small ads in the classified sections of the want ads in local papers should get you started. The quality of your work will often bring you enough business so you only have to advertise occasionally.

To learn this trade, check the courses offered at your local community colleges. You might also consider attending one of the following private schools which offer training in upholstering. Write or call them for their school catalog.

Florrisant Upholstery School
1408 North Kings Highway
St. Louis, MO 63113
Phone (314) 361-2852

FEGS Trade & Business School
62 W. 14th Street, 2nd Floor
New York, NY 10011
Phone (212) 741-7583

Hiram G. Andrews Center
727 Goucher Street
Johnstown, PA 15905
Phone (814) 255-5881

Perry Technical Institute
P.O. Box 9457
Yakima, WA 98909
Phone (509) 453-0374

Wyoming Technical Institute
Box 906
Laramie, WY 82070
Phone (307) 742-3776

CONTACT THIS ORGANIZATION REGARD-
ING MEMBERSHIP AND BENEFITS:

National Association of Professional
Upholsterers
200 South Main, P.O. Box 2754
High Point, NC 27261
Phone (919) 889-0113

Publish *Upholstering Today Magazine* and
numerous How-To-Books. 2794 members.

"There can be no self-discipline until one has experienced discipline and understood its merits."

Arendee

VIDEO TAPING BUSINESS

If you, or a member of your family does not presently have a video camera, it will take a few thousand dollars to get started in your own business, but this is another great business which you can start while working out of your home.

As with others we have described, small newspaper ads, a yellow page ad, and door-to-door solicitation will be necessary to begin this enterprise, but it can be very profitable.

Contact insurance agencies to tell them you are available to record a videotape of household goods, should any of their clients want it as proof of ownership in case of loss.

Contact Bridal shops and wedding counselors to let them know you videotape weddings and receptions.

Contact all fraternal organizations to let them know you record all parties, projects and parades.

Contact all hotels and motels which have meeting rooms. Tell them you are available to record prominent speakers and meetings.

Contact all golf shops. Let them know you can record any golfer's swing so he or she can work on improvement.

Use your own imagination to devise more uses for your services and you will make excellent earnings. As time goes on you continue to buy better equipment and have your own studio.

To start visualizing yourself in this business, call for an extensive free catalog of Video Cameras, Parts and Accessories offered by: MCM Electronics, 1-800-543-4330.

WATER PURIFICATION SYSTEM SALES AND SERVICE

There are many areas of this country where the water is not healthy to drink and/or tastes terrible. That is why we consider this business to be an excellent one to consider.

You can actually start your own business, be a manufacturer's representative, with as little as a few hundred dollars to start.

In our search for opportunities we could recommend, we found the Lufkin Company in Lufkin, Texas. Their advertising materials leave a great deal to be desired, but their products are good ones and they will set up independent dealers without requiring a substantial investment.

If you are the type of person who can supervise and motivate others, this business offers tremendous growth opportunities through hiring others to work for you.

Call or write for more information:

Lufkin Water Filters, Inc.
P.O. Box 151622
Lufkin, TX 75915-1622.
Phone (409) 634-5500.

CONTACT THIS ORGANIZATION REGARDING MEMBERSHIP AND BENEFITS:

Water Quality Association
4151 Naperville Road
Lisle, Illinois 60532
Phone (708) 505-0160

Among publications printed is a national directory of leading water conditioner dealers, manufacturers and suppliers. 2600 members.

WINDOW TINTING

This is a sensational business which is relatively new. Consequently, in most areas of the country you can establish a business out of your home and have absolutely no competition.

The best place to open this business is, of course, in one of those areas of the country which has more sun.

The business consists of applying a thin plastic film to any glass so that 97% of the ultraviolet radiation is deflected, glare and heat are reduced and both car seats and furniture placed near windows in homes are protected from fading.

For less than $300.00 you can get the know-how and starting materials to open your own business. You can begin immediately by going to your customers after running small ads in local papers. As soon as possible follow this up with an ad in the yellow pages. If you work hard and call on prospective customers such as furniture stores and restaurants, it won't be long before you can afford to have your own shop where you can work on cars.

Call or write:

Tropical Window Tinting
1612 Suncoast Boulevard
Homosassa, Florida 32646
Phone (904) 795-3456

Ask to speak with the owner: Karl LaFollette.

WINDOW WASHING AT SMALL SHOPPING CENTERS

Here's another business which can lead to some amazing profits which you can start for less than $100.00.

Get a copy of your local yellow pages and see if you can find a Janitor Supply or Maintenance Supply business.

When you find one, go there and buy some large squeegees, a double elongated pail set on rollers, a soft brush, a pole, some rags and a few bottles of ammonia and/or vinegar.

Load up your car with this equipment and drive to the first strip mall you come to. Walk into the first store and ask the proprietor if you can wash his (or her) windows. Offer to do it for a very small amount, say $1.00 per front window. If the person hesitates, offer to do it for nothing if you can fill your buckets with water. Chances are you will get a yes, and when you do simply say, "Would you do me a favor, though; please don't tell the other store owners that I did yours for nothing."

When finished with the first store, you go to the next store and say, "I just did the windows next door and they look great; can I do yours? Because it's Tuesday, (or whatever) I'll do them all for just $10.00."

Keep going like this from one store to the next. Each time you finish, ask if they are pleased. If they say yes, ask if you can return in a month to do them again. Then hand the person your card along with a receipt and instruct them to call you if they have any odd jobs which need to be done.

As soon as possible, get a phone answering machine at home if there is no one there at all times to answer.

Write everything down as the day goes on: names, addresses, phone numbers, even personal notes which can endear you to the person next time. For example, (has a son Jim who has the flu.) Do not try to remember everything at the end of the day. You won't.

Use self-discipline. Tell yourself that you can't go home until you earn a specific amount.

> **"Believe that life is worth living, and your belief will help create the fact."**
>
> **William James**

> *"I would give no thought of what the world might say of me, if I could only transmit to posterity the reputation of an honest man."*

Sam Houston

CHAPTER 4

SOURCES OF MORE INFORMATION AND ASSISTANCE

SOURCES OF MORE INFORMATION AND ASSISTANCE

The Importance Of Information

Information is power. It is an asset that can help overcome uncertainty and open new avenues for opportunity.

Success in business depends on what you know and how well you can apply what you have learned. With the right information, your business gains an important edge in today's competitive world.

Learn to use the following information sources. They are the key to unlocking your business's full potential.

FEDERAL INFORMATION RESOURCES:

The Small Business Administration

The SBA is an independent government agency created by Congress to help small businesses grow and prosper. The SBA has over 100 offices that offer small firms financial assistance through guaranteed loans, management assistance, help in obtaining government contracts, counseling services and many low-cost publications. The SBA is an excellent source of information.

Small Business Answer Desk
1-800-368-5855

This toll-free hotline provides personalized attention to your business needs. Provided by the SBA's Office of Advocacy, the ANSWER DESK is an excellent information and referral service. You're only one call away from improving your business. . . don't hesitate, phone today! In Washington, D.C. call 653-7561. The hotline operates from 8:30 am to 5:00 pm (EST), Monday through Friday.

SBA Publications

The SBA has over 100 business booklets that it sells for a small fee (most under $2.00). These publications address important business topics and answer the questions most frequently asked by prospective and existing small business owners. Get your free publications directory and order form by contacting either your local SBA Office or the SMALL BUSINESS ANSWER DESK.

Service Corps of Retired Executives (SCORE)

SCORE consists of over 12,000 business executives who volunteer their time to provide training and free management counseling to small business owners. SCORE's nationwide reputation for helping new and existing businesses is a result of their high-quality service.

Small Business Development Centers (SBDCs)

SBDCs are sponsored by SBA in partnership with state and local governments, the educational community and the private sector. They provide high-quality, low cost assistance, counseling and training to prospective and existing small business owners. There are over 500 SBDCs in 42 states.

Small Business Institute (SBI)

SBIs are operated through the SBA in every state on almost 500 college campuses across the nation. Over the course of a college semester, the institutes provide in-depth student and faculty counseling to select small business clients.

SBA District And Regional Offices

Most SBA offices maintain a "training calendar" to help business people locate appropriate training sessions and information. Consult the phone directory under U.S. Government, or call the SMALL BUSINESS ANSWER DESK at 1-800-368-5855 to locate the SBA office nearest you.

Department Of Commerce
Office Of Business Liaison (OBL)
The Office of Business Liaison provides information on business assistance programs offered by all Federal agencies. For a listing of U.S. Department of Commerce services, call 202-377-3176.

Economic Development Administration (EDA)
EDA assistance is available for areas experiencing high unemployment, low income quotas or sudden and severe economic distress. Call 202-377-5113 for more information.

The Minority Business Development Agency (MBDA)
MBDA provides management and technical assistance to business owners and, in general, encourages financial support for minority-owned firms. Look under U.S. Government in your local telephone directory or call the SMALL BUSINESS ANSWER DESK to find the MBDA office nearest you.

International Trade Administration (ITA)
ITA's office of U.S. and Foreign Commercial Service maintains a vast data base of up-to-date foreign market information and assists in establishing foreign market contacts. Call 202-377-1289 for more information.

Internal Revenue Service
For more information on your Federal tax obligations, go the local office of the Director of Internal Revenue Services. An excellent booklet (revised from year to year) on this subject is *Tax Guide for Small Business*, prepared by the Internal Revenue Service.

STATE INFORMATION RESOURCES:
State Economic Development Agencies
Most states have agencies that promote economic growth within the state by helping the state's

businesses grow and by encouraging outside firms to relocate in the state. These agencies are a valuable source of information on business opportunities, markets and state and local business assistance programs. Check your phone directory under Government, (State), for Economic or Industrial Development Agencies.

LOCAL INFORMATION RESOURCES:
City or County Development Agencies
Like most states, many local governments have their own development agencies that help small businesses in their jurisdiction.

Schools
Local colleges are an excellent source of business information. Most colleges offer courses in entrepreneurship, business management and other disciplines helpful to the small business owner.

The Library
Your local library is a virtual gold mine of information. . . use it. Most libraries have a business section and there is usually someone available to assist you in finding the specific information you need.

Business Periodicals
Information on most business topics can be found in a business periodical. These magazines and newspapers are a great source for up-to-date business news, recent technological developments, new marketing and management techniques, finance and related subjects. To find the article you need, look in the Business Periodical Index at your local library. *The Readers' Guide to Periodical Literature* is another excellent source for locating small business articles.

Chambers of Commerce

Most cities and towns have a Chamber of Commerce. These organizations promote the interests of local business owners and serve to stimulate business activity throughout their jurisdiction. Your local Chamber is an excellent source for information about local markets, business activity and business opportunities.

Banks

Many bank officers have a broad understanding of finance, business operations and the local economic climate. Do not be afraid to ask your banker questions.

> # "Who dares nothing, need hope for nothing."
>
> **Johan von Schiller**

CHAPTER 5

SELECTING THE BEST TYPE OF BUSINESS STRUCTURE

A Partnership Agreement Should Include The Following:

1. Type of business.
2. Amount invested by each partner.
3. Division of profit or loss.
4. Compensation for each partner.
5. Distribution of assets on dissolution.
6. Duration of partnership.
7. Provisions for dissolving.
8. Provisions for withdrawals or admission of additional partners.
9. Dispute settlement clause.
10. Restrictions of authority - expenditures.
11. Settlement in case of death or incapacitation.

Advantages	Disadvantages
Two heads better than one. Additional sources of venture capital. Better credit rating than corporation of similar size.	Death, withdrawal or bankruptcy of one partner. Difficult to get rid of bad partner. Hazy line of authority. Growth inhibited.

Corporation

You can incorporate without an attorney, but you would be unwise to do so. You may think a small family corporation does not need an attorney, but an attorney can save members of a family corporation from hard feelings and family squabbles. Attorneys' fees may run high if organization problems are complex. The corporate form is usually the most costly to organize.

Advantages	Disadvantages
Limited liability for stockholders.	Heavier taxes.
Continuity.	Power limited by charter.
Transfer of shares.	Less freedom of activity.
Change in ownership need not affect management.	Much legal formality.
Easier to raise capital.	Expensive to launch.

S Corporation (formerly known as Subchapter S)

Provisions allow shareholders to absorb all corporate income or losses as partners and report it as individual taxpayers. In essence, the S corporation is not affected by corporate income taxes, thereby eliminating the double taxation feature of standard corporations. Aside from being treated as a partnership from a tax standpoint, the S corporation and standard corporation share most of the same pros and cons, with a few exceptions.

The Corporation must meet certain requirements before the S corporation alternative becomes feasible. They are:

1. The corporation must be a domestic entity (incorporated within the United States).
2. The corporation can only have one class of stock.
3. Only individuals or estates can be shareholders.
4. The corporation cannot be part of another organization.
5. There is a maximum number of shareholders allowed.
6. The corporation cannot have any nonresident alien shareholders.
7. 20 percent or more of its revenue must be domestically generated.

8. Dividends, interests, royalities, rents, annuities and securities transactions cannot account for more than 20 percent of total revenues.

Control of the Business

Sole Proprietorship - You have absolute authority over all business decisions.

Partnership - Control of the business is shared with your partners which may lead to disputes. A partnership agreement could be helpful in solving possible disputes. However, you still are responsible for your partner's business actions, as well as your own.

Corporation (Standard or S) - Control depends on stock ownership. In other words, 51% stock ownership or control means that you are able to make policy decisions. Control is exercised through regular board of directors meetings and annual stockholders meetings. Records must be kept to document decisions made by the board of directors. Small, closely-held corporations can operate more informally, but record keeping cannot be eliminated entirely. Officers of a corporation can be liable to stockholders for improper actions.

CHAPTER 6

PREPARATION OF A BUSINESS PLAN

PREPARATION OF A BUSINESS PLAN

Planning:

If you don't know where you are going, you will end up somewhere else. Think about that!

Suppose you lived in Boston and decided to drive to Dallas; would you use a map? Of course you would. But what would happen if you didn't? It would be a very long, hard, trip and if you didn't know your geography, you probably would not make it to Texas, never mind Dallas.

Starting or running a business without proper planning is like driving from Boston to Dallas without a map. Planning will show you your destination and the best road to get you there.

This information summary will provide you with an overview of planning and discuss how and why to prepare a business plan.

Why Planning Is Critical:

- Planning gives you a path to follow. It makes your future what you want it to be.
- It is the most important guide to starting, building and managing a successful business.
- It is the best tool available to help a small business raise money.
- A business plan can be a communications tool for investors, suppliers, employees and others interested in understanding the operations and goals of your business.
- If you don't plan for the success of your business...you will fail. It is that simple!

Planning Can Be Difficult:

Although planning is critical to your success, it is often overlooked in favor of intuition or "gut feeling."

There are other obstacles that hinder planning, including:

- **Lack of know-how** — it is sometimes difficult to know how to plan and what to plan for.
- **Fear of the unknown** — it is hard enough dealing with the problems of today without worrying about what's going to happen in the future.
- **Inexactness** — the best set plans have a funny way of not working out exactly the way they are supposed to.

These obstacles are very real. However, they must be overcome if you are to be successful. While we may find it difficult to face the future, heading into it without any direction is much worse.

The Business Plan:

The business plan is a written document that clearly defines the goals of a business and outlines the methods for achieving them. A business plan describes what a business does, how it will be done, who has to do it, where it will be done, why it's being done and when it has to be completed. Dreams and ambitions are great and important. But what really counts in the business world are results. Therefore, it is important to establish realistic goals with a sound methodology for achieving them. A business plan:

- Is the management and financial "blueprint" for a business start-up and profitable operation.
- Is written by the business owner with outside help as needed.
- Explains how the business will function and depicts its operational characteristics.
- Details how the business will be capitalized and managed.

ELEMENTS OF A BUSINESS PLAN:

1. **Business Description**
   - Business name, address and owner indentification.
   - Identifies goals and objectives. Clarifies why you are or why you want to be in business.

2. **Products and Services**
   - Very descriptive explanation of all products and services.
   - Describes what you are selling and why.

3. **Sales and Marketing**
   - Sales and marketing are the core of your business rationale. Your plan should address several basic questions.
   - Who and how large is your market? How will you be competitive? What pricing and sales terms are you planning? How will you market your products and services?

4. **Operating Requirements**
   - The plan should identify and describe the equipment, facilities and people necessary to generate your products and services.
   - How will your products and services be produced and made available to the customer?

5. **Financial Management**

   This is the most critical part of your business plan. You will establish vital schedules that will guide the financial health of your business.

   If you are just starting a business, your plan should include:

   - Projected "start-up costs."
   - Your expected profit or return on investment (ROI) for the first year.
   - Projected income statement and balance sheet for two years.

- Projected monthly cash flow statement for 12 months.

If you are a young or established business, your plan should include:
- Income statement and balance sheet for the last two years.
- Projected income statement and balance sheet for the next two years.
- Projected monthly cash flow statement for 12 months.

Your plan should include an explanation of all projections. If you feel that your finance or accounting knowledge is not sufficient to prepare these statements, get professional assistance.

The bottom line is: will or does your company make a profit?

6. Concluding Narrative
This segment of your plan should summarize your business goals and objectives and send a message that you are committed to the success of your business.

Put Your Best Foot Forward:
Your business plan should be complete, clear, neat and accurate, It will be an extension of you and your business.

The length of a good plan will vary from a few pages to well over a hundred pages. The plan should provide a sound "blueprit" for your business and entice any reader to want to know more.

A Final Word On Planning:
Planning is the most important part of starting and running a successful business. It is a fact. . . if you don't know where you are going, you will end up somewhere else.

PREPARE YOUR BUSINESS PLAN

No matter what the business or its degree of complexity, the business person needs a **comprehensive plan** to translate his or her vision into a working operation. A business plan is best developed before you start operating your business and is prepared to provide completeness in planning a new business, present to a lending institution for a financial loan, promote an existing business in seeking additional investors for expansion, and assist management in determining areas of strength and weakness in making long-range business plans.

An outline of a model business plan follows. Possibly no plan would include all the items as listed; however, the more complete the plan, the more effective it is as a financial or management tool.

Outline of a Model Business Plan

1. **Cover letter or summary statement**
   a. Business description: name, location, product, years in business (if any).
   b. Business goals: short range (profit) and long range (expansion and growth).
   c. Loan requested: total cost of new venture or expansion, percent of total needed to borrow, terms and interest rate desired.
   d. Return on investment: net effective cash flow return per year over total investment.
   e. Equity structure: total ownership (equity investment) divided by total capitalization (total assets). A one-to-one ratio or a 50 percent equity is desirable.

2. **Uses and sources of funds**
   a. List uses or costs: land, building, equipment, and current operating costs for first two to six months.

b. List sources of funding: projected amount of total capital to be received from local bank, SBA, or venture capitalists, investment of cash and assets of major investors, and amounts invested by limited partners or stock investors.

3. **Personal information**
   a. Personal resumes of all major investors or owners.
   b. Personal average monthly budget of all owners.
   (List source of personal income, and typical monthly expenses).
   c. Current (within 60 days) balance sheet for each owner. List current value of all personal assets and personal debts.
   d. Copies of income tax returns (Form 1040) for the past three years.

4. **Management team**
   a. Copy of legal form of ownership (articles of partnership, corporation charter, etc.).
   b. Brief resumes and job description of key personnel: background, skills, duties.
   c. An organizational chart of the business.

5. **Legal documents**
   a. Lease agreements or purchase agreement.
   b. Franchise agreements, if any.
   c. Plans, specifications, cost breakdowns (if a building project).
   d. Business life insurance policy summary.
   e. Buy-sell agreements (insurance).
   f. Copies of licenses, zoning changes, fictitious trade name.
   g. Current credit report on owners from local credit bureau.

6. Market analysis - total projected sales for the next three years based on:
  a. Customers: group by common indentifiable characteristics. Who are they and where are they? Are they influenced by price, quality, service, personalities?
  b. Market size: state size of total market in both units and dollars; state portion of region and local market for this business.
  c. Competition: assess strengths and weaknesses of competitive products and services; describe how new business will have an advantage over competition in meeting special local needs.
  d. Future trends: whether ascending, descending or static demands, and degree of change.

7. Product or service
  a. Give physical description of product and service; how different from competition.
  b. A brief development history of product, including patents and copyrights.
  c. List vendor and source suppliers.

8. Physical plant
  a. Map of area and site location.
  b. Building layout showing product or customer flow.

9. Manufacturing process (if applicable)
  a. Raw materials, component parts, goods in process.
  b. Methods used in process.

10. Marketing strategy
  a. Describe general marketing philosophy.
  b. State product features emphasized: quality, service warranty, etc.
  c. State method of prospecting for customers.

d. Pricing and credit policies; relationship of turnover and margin.

e. Distribution policies: direct, wholesale, or mail; salesmen commission structure.

f. Promotion methods to be used: media, approaches, logo or trademark.

11. Financial feasibility

a. A brief, five year financial history, if existing business.

b. Financial pro forma statements:
- cash flow statement-- first year by months, and annual for next two years.
- income statement--for each of the first three years.
- balance sheet--for opening day and end of the first and second years.

c. Key business ratios--opening day and end of the first year.

d. Break-even chart

e. Anticipated major capital investments within the first three years.

f. A capitalization statement of worth of business on net income rate of return.

CHAPTER 7

STEPS TO TAKE
TO GET AN SBA
GUARANTEED LOAN

STEPS TO TAKE TO GET AN SBA GUARANTEED LOAN

1. Describe in detail the type of business to be established. (Your business plan)
2. List your business education, experience, and management capabilities.
3. Prepare an estimate of how much you or others have to invest in the business and how much you will need to borrow.
4. Prepare a current, signed, personal financial statement of the owner(s).
5. Prepare a projected profit and loss statement for the first year the business will operate.
6. List collateral to be offered as security for the loan. List the market value of each item.
7. Take this material with you and see your banker and ask for a direct bank loan. If the loan application is denied, ask the bank to make the loan under SBA's loan guaranty program. If the bank is interested in an SBA guaranty loan, ask the banker to contact SBA and discuss your application with them. In most cases of guaranty loans, SBA will deal directly with the bank.

CHAPTER 8

DECIDING WHERE
YOUR BUSINESS
WILL BE

DECIDING WHERE YOUR BUSINESS WILL BE

Deciding on the business you want to go into doesn't mean much unless you begin your life as an entrepreneur in a location where there are customers for your business.

The ideal location would be one where you have no competition and yet many people who need and want your products or services and can afford them.

If the neighborhood where you presently reside offers very little opportunity, then be realistic. Seriously consider moving to a new city, state, or country.

If a fresh start in a new location sounds good to you, consider every aspect of your move before pulling up stakes. Impulsive decisions made without forethought are often regreted.

Go for a visit if possible. If not, then start writing and calling. Begin by contacting the Chamber of Commerce.

If you have acquaintances in the city of your destination, ask them to find out what competition exists, and to let you know about: cost of living, available housing, state taxes, weather, public transportation, social and cultural activities, and the stability of the population.

The fastest-growing metropolises between now and the year 2000, according to the U.S. Department of Commerce, are:

1.) West Palm Beach, FL   5.) San Diego, CA
2.) Phoenix, AR   6.) Sacramento, CA
3.) Orlando, FL   7.) Tampa, FL
4.) Riverside, CA

The states which will have population increases of more than 36% are as follows:

Florida	Colorado
Texas	Wyoming
Arizona	Idaho
Nevada	Oregon
Utah	Washington

The states which will have a population increase of from 19% to 36% are as follows:

Georgia	Arkansas
South Carolina	Oklahoma
Virginia	New Mexico
Kentucky	California
Vermont	Montana
New Hampshire	Alaska
Louisiana	Hawaii

The states which will have population increases of one person to 19% are as follows:

Maine	Mississippi
New Jersey	Missouri
Delaware	Kansas
Maryland	Nebraska
West Virginia	Iowa
Indiana	Wisconsin
North Carolina	Minnesota
Tennessee	North Dakota
Alabama	

These states are expected to have a decline in population:

New York	Ohio
Massachusetts	Michigan
Connecticut	Illinois
Rhode Island	South Dakota
Pennsylvania	

Before you go anywhere, just make sure you do some heavy thinking. If you are working outside, perhaps you will do better in a warmer climate. If you are selling water purification units, go where the water is terrible. If you are going to clean carpets, don't move to Tent City. If you like the window tinting business go where the sun almost always shines. Get the idea?

Just make sure you don't get too comfortable sitting and thinking.

This country is full of people who sit on bar stools every day, drinking up their social security checks while telling whomever will listen how they could have been rich if it weren't for the fact they "never got the breaks."

Go make your breaks.

Do it today!

ABOUT THE AUTHOR

Richard Diggs is widely recognized for his contributions to the vocational sector of American education. A product of Detroit's parochial system and the University of Detroit, he has worked in numerous diverse positions which have included being a stock broker, bank department manager, night club comedian, college director, magazine editor and freelance writer.

In addition, Mr. Diggs has owned ten very distinct corporations including several proprietary occupational schools, an advertising agency, two retail operations, a manufacturing company, a business consulting firm and a publishing company.

Since 1965 Mr. Diggs has devoted almost all of his time to some aspect of post-secondary education. He was twice elected President of The Michigan Association of Private Schools, served on The Advisory Council on Adult & Continuing Education for the State of Michigan, and served for years on The Governor's Commission of Higher Education.

Mr. Diggs served as a member of the accrediting commission for The National Association of Trade & Technical Schools from 1972 through 1978, was Education Officer for the Region 5 Executive Committee of HEW under Dr. Mousolite, and founded The Michigan Organization of Private Vocational Schools.

Married with three children, Mr. Diggs is an acclaimed public speaker and author. In addition to *Keeping Students from Dropping Out*, first published in 1978, he wrote *Michigan's Private Occupational Schools* (1975), and seven books on the science of getting a job. These have included *Getting the Job You Want at the Wage You Know You Deserve* (1968), *The Great Job Hunt* (1985), *Employability . . . Plus* (1987), *Finding Your Ideal Job* (1988), and *Finding Your Ideal Job In The World of Electronics* (1990)

INDEX

A

B

C

D

E

F

G

H

I

J

K

L

M

M (Continued)

N

O

P

T

U

V

W

XYZ